FORMS FOR

How To

Find A Job

Where You Will

Never Work Again

Copyright Notice

Forms For
How To Find A Job Where You Will Never Work Again

by Richard Havenport.

© 1995 – 2018 Richard Havenport

All rights reserved. No portion of this book may be reproduced in any form without permission from the publisher, except as permitted by U.S. copyright law.

Dedication

This is dedicated to Jeffrey Long who encouraged me to be all that I could be. He was the first manager that I could say I admired and re-ignited my faith that there are good managers out there that care about their job and the employees that report to them.

Instructions

This book has been priced as a companion to the ebook "How To Find A Job Where You Will Never Work Again." You will need to buy the ebook in order to work with these forms. The forms are designed for each section of the ebook to help you track your progress which will also allow you to keep all your work in one place for future reference. It can be a guide to keep you on track with your goals or be an inspiration when you need to modify your goals in the future.

The workbook, along with these forms, is a life long goal that will help you be successful in your career and life. It can be a guide throughout your life that will be beneficial to you at any stage of you life.

At the end of this book there are a couple of notes pages for your convenience while reading the ebook.

Goals:
Family

Goals: Education		

Goals: Retirement		

Goals:
Career

Goals: Other		

Self Assessment Form

Your Name: _____   Marital Status: _____

| Age: _____ | Years of College: _____ | Goals: Family, Security, Career, Retirement, Other: _____ |

Jobs and Skills	Hobbies / Sports	Activities / Interests

Self Assessment Form

Continued

Jobs and Skills	Hobbies / Sports	Activities / Interests

Self Assessment Form

Continued

Jobs and Skills	Hobbies / Sports	Activities / Interests

Self Assessment Form - Students

Your Name: _____   Marital Status: _____

Age: _____

Goals: Family, Security, Career, Retirement,
Other: _____

Courses and Skills	Hobbies / Sports	Activities / Interests

Self Assessment Form - Students

Continued

Courses and Skills	Hobbies / Sports	Activities / Interests

Self Assessment Form - Students

Continued

Courses and Skills	Hobbies / Sports	Activities / Interests

Job / Course Skill Breakdown

Job / Course Title

List every skill gained on your job or course.

Job / Course Skill Breakdown

Job / Course Title

List every skill gained on your job or course.

Job / Course Skill Breakdown

Job / Course Title

List every skill gained on your job or course.

Job / Course Skill Breakdown

Job / Course Title

List every skill gained on your job or course.

Self Assessment Form

Mix and Match

Jobs/Courses and Skills	Hobbies / Sports	Activities / Interests

Self Assessment Form

Mix and Match - Continued

Jobs/Courses and Skills	Hobbies / Sports	Activities / Interests

List of Colleges, Universities, Technical Schools

This is a scratch pad for you to list all educational opportunities that are available to you.

Name:	Name:
Address:	Address:
City, State, Zip:	City, State, Zip:
Phone Numbers:	**Phone Numbers:**
Admissions:	Admissions:
Registrars:	Registrars:
Information:	Information:
Name:	Name:
Address:	Address:
City, State, Zip:	City, State, Zip:
Phone Numbers:	**Phone Numbers:**
Admissions:	Admissions:
Registrars:	Registrars:
Information:	Information:
Name:	Name:
Address:	Address:
City, State, Zip:	City, State, Zip:
Phone Numbers:	**Phone Numbers:**
Admissions:	Admissions:
Registrars:	Registrars:
Information:	Information:
Name:	Name:
Address:	Address:
City, State, Zip:	City, State, Zip:
Phone Numbers:	**Phone Numbers:**
Admissions:	Admissions:
Registrars:	Registrars:
Information:	Information:
Name:	Name:
Address:	Address:
City, State, Zip:	City, State, Zip:
Phone Numbers:	**Phone Numbers:**
Admissions:	Admissions:
Registrars:	Registrars:
Information:	Information:

List of Contacts

This is a complimentary form for listing any and all contacts you've made while researching your new career. Networking is an invaluable asset that one should always nurture in any career search.

Name:	Name:
Address:	Address:
City, State, Zip:	City, State, Zip:
Home Phone	Home Phone
Cell:	Cell:
Work:	Work:
Email:	Email:
Name:	Name:
Address:	Address:
City, State, Zip:	City, State, Zip:
Home Phone	Home Phone
Cell:	Cell:
Work:	Work:
Email:	Email:
Name:	Name:
Address:	Address:
City, State, Zip:	City, State, Zip:
Home Phone	Home Phone
Cell:	Cell:
Work:	Work:
Email:	Email:
Name:	Name:
Address:	Address:
City, State, Zip:	City, State, Zip:
Home Phone	Home Phone
Cell:	Cell:
Work:	Work:
Email:	Email:

Notes:

Notes:

Notes:

Notes:

Your Certificate

I am including a certificate of completion for you to fill out. This should be the most important certificate you will ever receive. This represents the work that you did for yourself, independently, on your own, which shows the responsibility that you have taken to better yourself as an individual. No one will ever give you credit for this. Yet, this will be one of the most important things you do in your life.

It is very possible that you will have a number of jobs be identified as potential careers. Rank them from the best on down and list them on your certificate in order. This will allow you to take advantage of any opportunity that is made available in the future.

Certificate of Completion

I hereby certify that I,

_____,

have completed the ebook workbook to the best of my ability and that from this day forward I am taking charge of my life.

I have found that the jobs that I enjoy and will find fulfillment in are

_____

_____

_____

_____

_____

Congratulations!

You've completed your search for the dream job that you always wanted.

www.ingramcontent.com/pod-product-compliance
Lightning Source LLC
Chambersburg PA
CBHW080629220526
45467CB00011B/3436